THE SPRING OF DREAMS

Selected Poetry and Prayers

Richard Rudd

With drawings and paintings by Jane Adams

First edition published in Great Britain and USA 2021
by Gene Keys Publishing Ltd
Lytchett House, 13 Freeland Park
Wareham Road, Lytchett Matravers, Poole BH16 6FA

Richard Rudd

THE SPRING OF DREAMS

Selected Poetry and Prayers

With drawings and paintings by Jane Adams

Hardback Print Edition ISBN 978-1-913820-01-5
eBook/Kindle/Apple Books Edition ISBN 978-1-913820-09-1

genekeys.com

CONTENTS

יהוה

ABOUT THE AUTHOR

Richard Rudd is an international teacher, writer and award-winning poet. His mystical journey began early in life when he experienced a life changing state of spiritual illumination over 3 days and nights in his twenties. Richard gained a Master's in literature and metaphysics from the University of Edinburgh. He has travelled extensively around the globe, sailing across the Atlantic at a young age and exploring the Pacific, the Americas, the Far East and the Arctic. Richard has a love of sailing and his family own and sail one of the few remaining Norfolk Wherries. Richard always had a love of the poetic and in 1996 his poem *The Siren Lovers* was awarded the prestigious FISH poetry award in Ireland. Richard is also founder of the Gene Keys, a synthesis of world wisdom followed by a large global community. He lives in Devon in the UK with his wife and family.

THE VISIONARY ART OF JANE ADAMS

I invited Jane Adams to illustrate this special book of poems and prayers, mainly because Jane is one of the deepest contemplators of the mysteries I have ever known. Jane uses art alongside her own words to probe the higher reaches of the wordless. Of the illustrations in this book, some were created intentionally to sit along with the writings, whereas others come from her own extensive repertoire. Her ability to dance with a brush, pen or crayon knows no bounds…Sometimes she loves to trace logical patterns of geometry, time and space and at others she delights to dive fearlessly into the mystic and the mythic. You can easily feel her playful, nature-loving spirit when you look at her artwork and I feel very proud to have my words sit alongside her art.

Richard Rudd

To find out more about Jane's amazing body of work, you can visit her at janeadamsart.wordpress.com

FOREWORD

The art of poetry needs to be distinguished clearly from the business of writing poems. Almost anyone can write a poem. Far fewer people understand poetry as an art. You need never write a single line of poetry to have the heart of a poet. You simply need to live your life poetically. To live poetically is to learn to live slowly, to be still and to draw upon life's secret fire – in the landscape, in your surroundings, in people's hearts and in the daily challenges of mortality.

Sometimes however, living poetically also leads to the reaction of a poem. For me, true poems are not consciously written – rather they detonate at certain points in one's life. They explode out of us like springs forcing their way out of the depths of the unconscious earth into the sparkling light of day. Such poems have no clear set of rules. They may have structure or they may discard all structure. They may be lyrical, colloquial, rhyming, humorous or prosaic.

The one thing a true poem has is a sense of the mysterious.

I have chosen the poems in this small volume for this one quality – because I feel they each possess something that my mind cannot quite understand. They each somehow surpass me. I therefore encourage you to read them in this way – as you might listen to a bird singing. Afterwards you may think to yourself – I wonder what that means? In this way, the poems can burrow into your heart and soul, bypassing your mind. Such is the wonder of poetry.

The prayers in Part 2 of this book are obviously very different from the poems. Both poetry and prayer dance along the banks of the wordless realm. I believe that prayer goes even further than poetry. Prayer uses the word as a vehicle for the heart and soul to ride on. Prayer must be uttered. It can be uttered internally or it can be sounded out loud. It is an ancient form of transformational magic. All the prayers in this book came to me from a feminine spirit, as though dictated. I have worked with and around words for my whole life, but never have I felt more of an empty vessel than when I was receiving these prayers. I hope they will bring more light into your life, as they have done my own.

Richard Rudd
November 2017

RICHARD RUDD

THE POEMS

THE SIREN LOVERS

The Sea heaves at me
and I heave back,
there is a tension there
that would shatter atoms
fire fish skyward
like tendrils of light
scything a black sky.

White brows frown
from gull-clipped crags
in the old man's face.
He peers at me, jeers
and coils like a cat
folding my life forever
between two giant silken paws.

I see her too,
vicious, tireless Sculptress
weaving her webbed waves
about his breath,
and teasing a pounding pulse
between the shores of her lips
she lends him her ecstasy.

Together they lie.
He, with his brigand's smile
finite in the foam
combs her hair, unaware
that his great life lies
in the wind that she blows
across a single upturned palm.

Outright Winner of the 2006 FISH International Poetry Prize

THE SPRING OF DREAMS

Liquid words slap the sides of my skull
as I shovel the bones of bygone days
into the furnace of time.
Above in the forest the fireflies blaze,
fizzing in a haze that mostly resounds
to the ghostly psalms of owls.

I take up my staff, uncoiling, and quietly I part the night

A forest-fire of visions gathers in my eyes
and volleys of arrows,
dipped in charms, loosed
as loping shadows
sever the night with strange songs.

I see a stallion struggling in a spider's web,
a panther's breath burning my ear,
and the earth sucking at my feet,
now hands lifting me free,
the flicker of a face
then darkness, night.

A child crying, a bird dying, an old man I know,
the echoes of eagles behind the moon,
the sounds fish make under the sea
and my mother's face inside a tortoise shell
with stars as eyes …

A child seems to peer from between my eyes
a child looking at a child
one swaying with willows in his gaze
melting almost in a noise of flames and steam
and tears on his tongue
the other stone-spun –
suffering a daze of objects
and a silent sundial stare on his face.

Through this cranium, light performs:
double-back, open-fired flick-flack sighs,
in a mess that hurts my eyes
and screams about my mind,
kicking open doors to flaming carpets, splintering locks,
and hurls from windows dusty clocks
into a huge pile of stopped thoughts -
a smouldering heap beneath a gardener's fork.

His crooked browning cloak he weaves,
half-hid amongst the golden leaves
and all about, echoes of his heart
rocket us into the Garden dream.

Pitchfork paths and primrose hearths
spatter the softening sapling dew
and somewhere ahead, we can hear his bells;
snowdrop chimes dripped from his lips
and the yawn of a solitary oak.

Ah, Yes. The gushing spring of dreams is sprung at last
and flowers, eyelids in the earth
blink their birth at the blueing sky,
and I …

I hold the trees in my arms and squeeze
and lick the leaves from my palms...

8

THE KEEPSAKE

A dusky, serene summer's eve in a dream

the dalliance of moths

in a copper-cloth sky

I climb the jagged air

as a rose-milk moon

rises in a locket across your breast.

I hold your heart close;

a keepsake

framed by marsh marigolds.

WALK WITH A FRIEND

Stony days, and cold,
where the wind moves in close,
buried in eddies and tight circles
cut by a surgeon's sacred knife,
opening the skin on the world.

Tucked in a day
where the dry rain drizzles
through a half-cut beard
and drips to the earth in lonely drops,
and woods awash in our gentlest thoughts.

Calm under here, where the sea holds her breath
and steams her sweat
down the streaming, tinkling, salt licked bows
to be brushed from our brows
by a buttermilk hand.

Chaos out there, on the pink-cheeked beach
with the fearful whinny
of the deadweight waves …

and though our bodies
must shamble and wade this day,
our souls stride out,
tangling with the mist where the fulmar glides
and scrunching into shells where the hermit crab hides.

This mediaeval weather heaves us about,
makes candles burn in castles in windows in our eyes
and though not touching, our circumference lies
wider than the wind and the waves,
or the rain that dies...

THE VALLEY

I awoke with your tears upon my lips.
It wasn't calm, I didn't glide
but shook myself from my sleep
in a great black, serpentine scream
that tore through the crust of my dreams.

I was with your mother and your sister,
we talked of you and she seemed so sad, your mother.
It was not seeing you that hurt me so;
to talk of you with your own mother …
and she was so subtle, so feminine.

About you she told me nothing.
So much nothing that I heard something.

I can't help it, like a wave
you run, up and down my nervous system.
Your blood hurls through my veins,
I can taste your sweat, smell your earth.

I am trying to bridge it, this valley,
this valley that separates us.
The valley is the pain and the love.

For you to be so far for so long,
and then so near, closer even than this pain,
it judders my heart,
it sets me on top of you, beneath you,
it plunges me into you, through you …
I am trying to be you, all my life I am trying
to leave this pain …

But, I cannot.

You are not here now, you have gone.
What remains is some blessed seed
you must have let slip from your palm,
and now it moves, something moves in my breast,
only a little, but a little is a lot.

I am in love with the valley you see,
I am afraid to meet you, to be you.
Without you, there is no valley;
no green, no purling brooks, no swinging cows,
no worship.

If I meet you fully, I can no longer worship.
I am eaten up, swallowed whole,
if I meet you fully, I will lose.

THE HOLY-DAY

You simply cannot afford to miss this life.
You simply must not blink.
Rising with the sun,
I am the only one
gracious enough to unpeel my day.
Where are the thousands of others
come to greet the Dawn?
The banks of life should be lined
with mothers, fathers and their children
who rose excitedly in the dark,
packed picnics and frisbees and oranges
amidst whisperings and racing of hearts,
and, on an ordinary working day
came to the banks to play.

I declare every Single day
a Holy-Day.

And I, a strange young man,
tender you a prophecy …
that one crystal morning, just as this,
when the world is somehow quieter
and has time and chance for bliss,
that it shall come to pass
that children and their parents
who come to the banks to dance …
will arise before dawn,
and in the gentle sunlight of that day,
all strangers will embrace

And the whole world will never again miss another dawn.

For how can you possibly sleep
when you understand this Bliss?
You simply cannot blink,
and you never, never miss.

THE PUNCH LINE

Everyone … every one here
is lost and looking for home.
I fell on my arse
and everyone saw!

Once you've fallen down,
as long as you don't get up again
you can't fall again.
For pity's sake, just stay down!

It's so pleasant down here,
it's so nice and quiet.
I can see up all the girls' skirts!
I can see in all the boys' hearts.

We are all just wandering children.
The only time we actually really talk
is when two of us happen to fall on our arses
next door to each other,

and then, from our new vantage
we look up together laughing
at ourselves, at our good fortune
and the irony that those above, pity us!

and we pity them, that never fall
for they will only ever hear
the beginning of the joke
and miss the wonderful news
that our suffering is the punch line.

THE ARMADILLO

Where can you flee, old man,
too tired to dance
who sips the arc of aeons?

Volcanoed from the earth
and oiled on the anvil of your birth
you rose, dripping golden dust
to suck the milk of space.

One fleeting lick of blue
and you lowered your crumbling gaze
into a heresy of humbling red.
Here where the earth-smith waits
to twist your spine in shame
thus forging from its primal links
the matrix of your pain.

Your tears are your skies now,
your coracles of hope
that ripple on the shoulders
of that vast, dark nourishment.
Your tears are your stars now,
the flashing sapphire scintillae
in whose lenses you bathe
for the echo of your dream.

The King's hem quivers on the fool's cloak;
yours is a kiln of basalt hung across the night
a mantle of unfelt power.
Here crouched within his bones unheard
the windy hermit works
kissing embers orange from the fire,
he churns the world within your wound
and mutters in your eyes.

Strange, those moons of moving eyes …
their cold gleam cut upon a raven pond
mad with the dance of toads.
Sad, those earth-bent eyes;
their fearful hum
tempered in the belly of the world.

These are the eyes where we sit and wait
and open-mouthed receive
the great, bewildering ghost of man
whose mighty breath we dare not breathe.

THE MADMAN OF LITHIA

Ashland: Land of Gods

where the madman roams

amidst the pealing, drunken leaves

of the Lithia's golden cobweb-sheaves.

Who yawns the night, the blue-green night

and the endless, tireless echoing days

to plunge and sweep through the blue-cut night?

Weatherboard white and a rosebud hub

nettled in the dusky dream-lit eve,

a coltsfoot shire, with a yearning, leaning

sometime screaming rush of the Lyre,

I gamble my days in the dice-strewn stream

and squat upon the granite-flecked blocks

of the whispering moon-moths.

Lost upon these endless, lifting, silvering songs

floats the madman flinging his mad, mad dreams

and his moss-holed pockets heaving with Gods

and his moon-fire melting the hearts of those who sleep

beneath the soft cowl of the Lithia's green-gold shoals …

26

I AM NOT MY NAME

Bowling up the long green lane that leads to the Grey Wethers
the September ease dreaming its way
through my hair -
a sudden pungent mottle of fungi …

Stopping to scrawl these lines –
one by one as they come

a red-admiral flies encircled by cones
and a brown dab of sepia linnet smudges
the air with its song.

Distant gunfire almost spoils my reverie,
but the ancient moor ever bends its will
towards the warrior.

I am drawn to ponder those men who have walked this road before me -
the miner, the murderer, the poet, the priest …
I am no longer foolish enough to think
I am anyone,
nor that I was any of these, or could be again -
I am not my name.

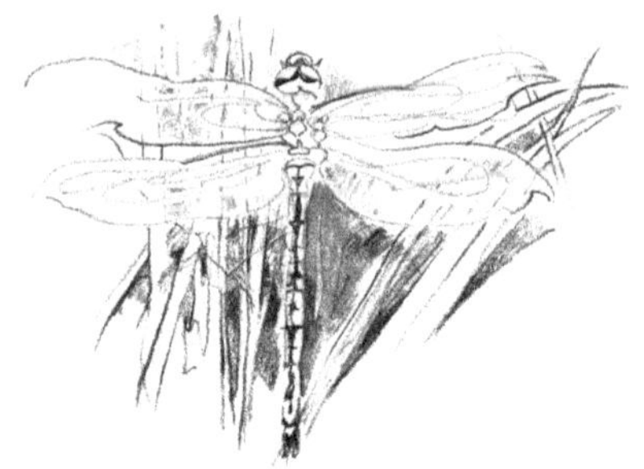

There are only these two striding legs hurling me on,
and my thoughts – fleeting as the mossy webs
that stitch together these pines.

I reach the threshold of the moor,
drop my baggage and leap down from a high wall
onto the moor
and words are instantly swallowed by its fathoms.
Quiet for some time now ... as thoughts begin to settle
and the poem enters deeper into my blood.

Twin circles of stone. Beautiful.
A moorland stream – I find myself naked, submerged in peat.
A dragonfly.

Drying in a warm autumn wind lying atop
an ancient clapper bridge.

Homewards via Manaton -
a stream and an oak wood
with a copper-haired artist in it -
his easel supporting my day

a dream-pool netted in beech-leaves
Deep, Cold, Pure.

Trickling water – I follow – a spring.
I pull away mud, deadwood, leaves
to reveal an opening under a rock –
a quartz citadel.
Flowers – lilac and yellow -
Today is my birthday.

A blessing and a prayer.

DALLIANCE

Everywhere you look, the birds are dancing.
The jackdaws in their inky hoods
Knocking each other off the chimney pots,
The mossy-eyed wrens kicking the leaves playfully
In their partner's little brown faces.
The pigeons too, are in on the gaming -
Parading their soft, round bellies
Like some strange marching band
Sighing through the Cypress trees.
Even the sparrow hawk, with his roving, rogue's eye
Forgets himself for a moment,
Puts aside his long, bloodstained lineage
To delight in a great sexy swoop,
That he hopes will not go unnoticed.

Who, when out among such theatricals,
Doesn't carry home at least a token
Of the gentle glow and glimmer
Of the unquenchable Hope of this world?

I WALKED...

I walked through the night-fields naked in the night ...
and the owl and the wainscot mouse did stare
at the winnowing man whose arse was bare,
for my chest was the Sultan commanding the stars,
two arms wheeling in the windmill of the night,
from the thrust of my penis, flung sparks of liquid fire,
an arched body curved like a rapier with delight.
The wheat-fire trembled with tongues of flames, like jewels ...
to wrench those red-hearts from their long-stuck sockets
down in the places where men do live.

The night will always be ours, to roam … naked 'midst the leaves,
and leave our dark thoughts to meet the wild ones there,
and soar, and shimmer, and lift the hair
on the necks of those safely tucked in bed.
Danger lives here, and the darting fox; surgeon of the Night,
peeling your heart with his ice-clear gaze,
he strips you to your shadows, and screams across your fears …

Eaves of wheat shall bow and lick your feet,
and the ears of the earth will echo with the sounds
of the spineless ones wriggling in the ground.
We inherit the dark space, the shadow, the grave,
out of it we burst, and slither from our pain,
go scurrying indoors, and shudder from our shame.
And yet it lives, our death in the woods of the night,
in the dens of our hearts and in the shafts
of our shouting night-cries,
when we brave our bliss
to hurtle through the gloom of our half dead kin
and minister the dark ones with a half-dead kiss …

I walked through the night-fields naked in the night
and the owl and the wainscot mouse did stare
at the winnowing man whose arse was bare,
with a chest filled with lightning, and the posture of a King,
a volcano for a penis, and the whole night to sing …
for think upon it Friend; wherefore do you stare?
Because while you thought of sleeping, I was really there.

THE ROOM

The Room seems so Silent

the Room of my dream.

The trail of a silver snail

that idled against the cold, stone wall

one sunny afternoon;

the silk-thread lives

of those who have pierced

this dawning room.

The breath left by a lizard

who wriggled through a tiny crack

in the brown oak panels,

eight years ago to this day.

Cobwebs by the thousand,

spun by thousands;

the lattice of thought

left over a hundred years of passers-by

through this room,

this life.

Finger-marks on the corners

of yellowed pages, notes-in-the-margin

now turned sour.

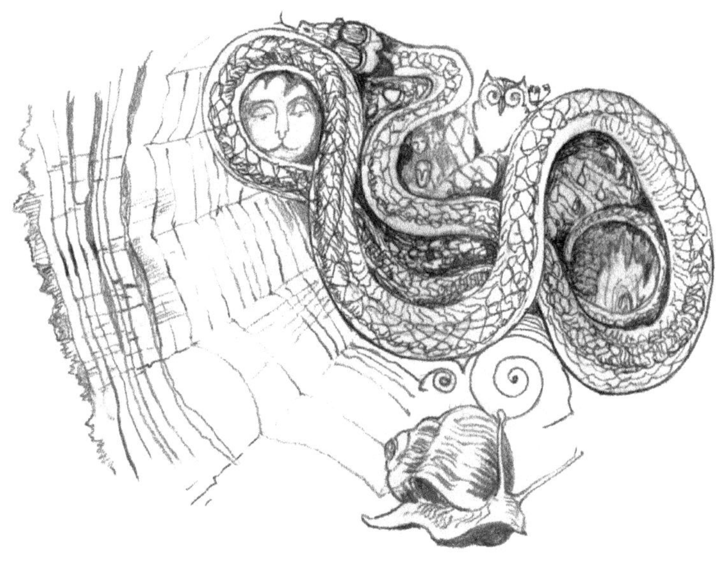

The builder's hands, the dirt in his nails
and the architect, and the Lord,
all leave their lives imprinted
in this tiny, hurtling room.
The thoughts and feelings
of their fathers and mothers
and the seed and dreams of the Great Grandmothers …
the claw of the dinosaur and the tooth of a star
linger here upon these dusty shelves …

There is no where,
where history does not lie coiled in its entirety,
no room, no plant, no drop of urine even,
from where the future does not watch us,
half amused, half disgusted;
half alive.

It is all in the waters.
Through our waters we lie,
curled in the One great round embrace.

The spirit and the heart of the poet
is reborn in the tears we shed
on hearing the atomic timbre
of the poem read aloud.

Only the waters remain.

Not a drop shall be lost and not a drop can be added.

There is only the relentless wind,

shaping and reshaping

the endless crystalline cells of our blood

across the golden dunes of our days …

Our secret, royal blood

keeper of the keys,

crimson crypt of information,

scripts, papyri, languages, stories and song,

sounds, pain, Silence and rain …

Here has lived and died the ancient turtle

or the tail and stream of a lion or a cloud.

Here sleeps the long dead mollusc …

In our blood lurks Evil

and the understanding of Evil.

In the blood hides God,

the Supernova,

and the tinkling Silence of the womb.

Every speck of dust,

every breath of moisture

must be heard

before we can see the insurmountable

breadth of our Mystery.

Before me is the image

of a coiled green snake

carved into the cold, stone wall

of the room in my Dream.

Only Through him flows the blood

cold enough to comprehend

the blistering sanctitude

of what we are given.

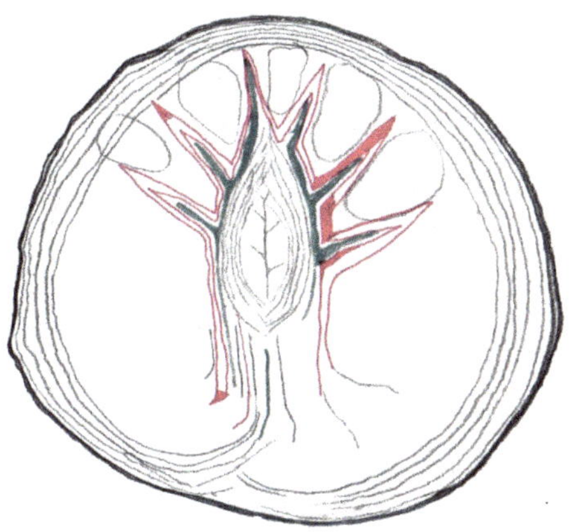

Only through him can we sense out the truth

encrypted in his scales

and in the mystery of that lolling mouth.

And His is the legacy of doom,

for he, and only he,

of all the beings who have flowed through this room

for countless days and days;

only He remains.

THE PASSING OF HU

*In memory of Ra Uru Hu
a great man and revered mentor*

He was a man
small in stature, wide in wonder,
who flung his guitar
with a flourish at the stars
and strung a net of pearls to ponder.

He dressed in dark clothes,
wore a dogged, dogtooth grin,
but his words and his eyes
rose fiery to the skies
scorched by the truth from within.

'I lived on a chair in a tree for a year'
was a favourite tale he retold.
He took his disdain,
swallowed his name
and he disappeared from the world.

He sung no songs of those savage days
and their wuthering, wide-eyed nights
but they looted his mind
and he lost his mind
in phantasmagorical heights.

Then one night, an awe-full night,
a great storm came to his being,
and who could have grasped
that he was the one, chosen to pass
through the eye of the Eye of all seeing?

Eight fateful days he hurtled
vagabond through the deeps,
outwit, outgunned, out-mastered
by intelligence surpassing
through a world that never sleeps.

This was no sylph of the southern skies,
no soft-voiced spirit in indigo cloak.
It was a darkling light,
black within white -
it was the formless Voice of the Form that spoke.

Emblazoned in embers from the iron-ore core
stepped the re-forged Hu,
dragging molten truth
Man's final truth -
end-time gift for a fractal few.

Years now slipped since that mystic flood
and the electric afterglow fades,
but his legend lingers,
and the music from his fingers
and the heart of the man pervades.

He was a man of crystal shores,
dark-edged corsair of the Balearic seas,
he trod the misty foam of earth
and left the gift of human worth;
Rauruhu – guest of gods – a gust on the breeze.

MY MOTHER

My mother was an island girl

with golden whorls and shell-shaped curls

that frothed and furled and seemed to me

to echo with the seasons of a sea-green sea.

Long running beach-running legs had she

honeyed by a hundred summering dreams of the sea

and a pair of piercing blues were set

in a face where the rivers of her friends had met.

My mother was the whole wide world -

when a boy from the shoals of his dreams was hurled,

by night on soft-set lioness paws she came,

and her voice was soft as a rose-petal rain.

And in those rising days of the laughing sap

my heaven and my haven was her rolling lap -

on waylaid waves the memories arise;

a boy and his mummy under pale parchment skies.

My mother was a friend to life,

doted upon, a devoted wife;

she wore her smile like an old straw hat

which I line with violets – she would have liked that.

It's easy to remember both the sweet and the good

but my mother was more – she had temper and mood -

impatience, yearning, will and passion;

she was roses and thorns, wind upon ocean.

Dear Mother, you are more than the memories lying on our shelves,

more than a dusty gathering gallery of selves;

a golden girl, a fine-figured lady,

a weathered old woman, a new-born baby.

These were but the passing texture of your days -

days that have passed now, but one thing that stays,

born from the passion that you brought from the start

is the friend-giving warmth of your life-living heart.

In her heart, my Mother was an island girl

with golden whorls and shell shaped curls

that frothed and furled and seemed to me

to echo with the seasons of a sea-green sea.

MY FATHER

My father was a generous man
Through life with gentle ease he flowed
And his deeds were the seeds he softly sowed,
A gardener-soul, he tended his hours
To yield a field of fragrant flowers.

My father was a diligent man
As a boy through upper meadows he stole
Planting his oaken dreams in our soul,
And in a land of gathering clouds and clay
his impeccable legacy illumines our way.

My father was an exceptional man

On the surface mild-mannered, he was modest and wise

Lived a life of great soul in delicate guise,

Of invisible virtues and stories untold

But beneath it he shimmered, vermilion gold.

My father was a daring man

Entreprenurial, an English pioneer

A gentleman racer beneath a gracious veneer

But his greatest mastery, truth to be told

Were the friendships he fostered all over the world.

My father was a thoughtful man

He placed others before him, devoted his life

To serving community, family and wife.

An anchoring presence, uncommon to rile

We cherish your solace and treasure your smile.

My father is a wonderful man

He lives now in our hearts, where his seeds are still growing

Imparting his wisdom with the same gentle knowing.

Humble and noble, you always see clearly

But we miss you and love you, so very, very dearly…

THE BALLAD OF COCK ROBIN

Cock Robin
Apple bobbin
Hood Robin Hood

Winter's hand
Fiery brand
Good Robin good

Frosty Walk
Private Talk
Spy, Robin spy

Gardener's fork
Sparrow-hawk
Fly, Robin fly

Holy wells
Wedding bells
Ring, Robin ring

Daffodils
Windowsills
Sing, Robin sing

Mother's love
Crooning dove
Go, Robin go

Father's arms
Misty farms
Flow, Robin flow

All is gone
Travelling on
Rise, Robin rise

Long lament
Elbows bent
Wise, Robin wise

Cock Robin
Apple bobbin
Hood Robin Hood

Cock Robin
Apple bobbin
Good, Robin good

HEADING NORTH

Heading north on autumn currents
  crepuscular Sunday drivers
    trawling the murmerless dawn
      stunned by the gaps in their thoughts.

  Up before dawn
  before the bronze rose grows
and glows through the muted marine fields
  of an unclaimed England.

PROVENANCE

The summer swallows farrow the clouds of my July.

A salvo of lofty lobs aimed far too high

and a singular, spectacular downpour

have drenched my dreams

and unfastened the stars from the sky.

They now occasionally wink at me

between the dirt in my toenails

Dear God please help me to find my provenance

Legs that tread the old paths around islands
must tread and tread again.
The ancient tramp of pilgrims' hopes
has cut these paths.
Now the falcon leans on cool, clean air
and birthdays come and go
riding September's tidal soul

Dear God please help me to find my provenance

Like an unhooked pendulum shot into the blue
the undulating line of life must fly
sailing 'till it lands and falling where I lie
face down in the green.
But on mossy, crumpled knees I rise,
cut a new staff to strike out again
into the brave horizon of winds

Dear God please help me to find my provenance

And when the rushy bracken folds up its days
and clings limply to the wheeling meadows
and the stricken leaves give up their
final sighs to winter loam
then the patient darkness beckons
my vagrant soul to come in at last
bringing an end to dreams
so, at last will I have earned my provenance.

KADO
(explorations into the zen way of poetry)

The wind on the water
sings with a face
of forgotten words

Lying beneath an oak
listening to the acorns drop
smiling hugely at the sky

All the way home
my bicycle meanders
through the songs of bees

The gate is closed.
Ravens river the air
above the carved brown earth

The Moon
shimmers brightly
across my precious heart

To reach the true rage
hum
while she is shouting at you

All along the roadside
the slugs are making
a break for it

The blackberry
borrows a hand
to return to its source

I take my shirt off –
the sun goes behind a cloud
for this!

*T*he footballers arrive
by van, bike and foot
the one on the bike scores

*D*amn
what do they put in the wine
in this bar, my heart?

THE PRAYERS

PRAYER OF TRANSMUTATION

Angels and Beings of the Pure Light,

please help me to purify and transmute

this dense, low frequency karmic energy

into Love, into Light, into Purity, into Truth,

into the spirit of Divine Tenderness.

PRAYER FOR ILLNESS

I call upon the great being we know as Raphael,

Archangel of Healing and Love.

Raphael, friend of all humans and all sentient creatures,

please bring your deep red-gold healing light into my body.

Let your warmth flow through the many subtle layers

of my energy body.

May you stitch up the rent in the fabric of my being.

May your light lead my intuition to the place

where healing is most needed.

May your radiance imbue me with vigour.

May your love inspire me with a quiet knowing

of the perfection of this illness.

May I learn greater compassion

through the gift of this suffering.

May I dedicate more of my being to the service of the whole.

I dedicate this suffering to the service and healing of the whole.

I hold you close for as long as I need you.

I thank you for the Grace of this suffering.

PRAYER OF DEEP SERENITY

Divine Mother, I come before you
naked and vulnerable.
Please allow me to enter
your sacred womb-space.
Please help me to settle into
the infinite peace of your arms.
Please bring me the deep, gentle patience
of the pregnant mother.
Everything happens at the perfect time.
Everything is for the great Good.
Please soften my heart and remind me
of my true home.

PRAYER OF MANIFESTATION
AND DIVINE SERVICE

Angels and Beings of the higher worlds,

please help me to bring this wish into form.

I ask this thing in order to align more deeply

with my higher purpose and so that I can be

of greater service to the whole.

Please help me to manifest the very highest possible potential

within the limitations of this form.

Purify my aura constantly

in order for higher forces to work through me.

I make my body, heart and soul

available for your pure emanations.

Make me an instrument of your Wisdom, your Love and your Truth.

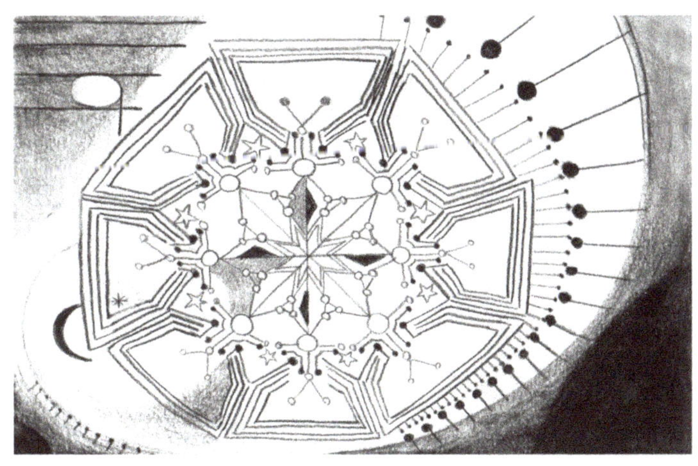

4
Causal
2
Astral
3
Mental
7
Monad
5
Buddha
6
Atma
1
Physical

RAINBOW BLESSING OF THE ARCHANGELS

Mikhael, Angel of Divine Will,
bless my physical body
with the Ray of Incandescence

Khamael, Angel of Omniscience,
bless my astral body
with the Ray of Phosphorescence

Raphael, Angel of Universal Love,
bless my mental body
with the Ray of Rubescence

Haniel, Angel of Epiphany,
bless my causal body
with the Ray of Iridescence

Tsadkiel, Angel of Forgiveness,
bless my buddhic body
with the Ray of Pearlescence

Gabriel, Angel of Truth,
bless my atmic body
with the Ray of Quiescence

Tsaphkiel, Angel of Grace,
bless my monadic body
with the Ray of Luminescence.

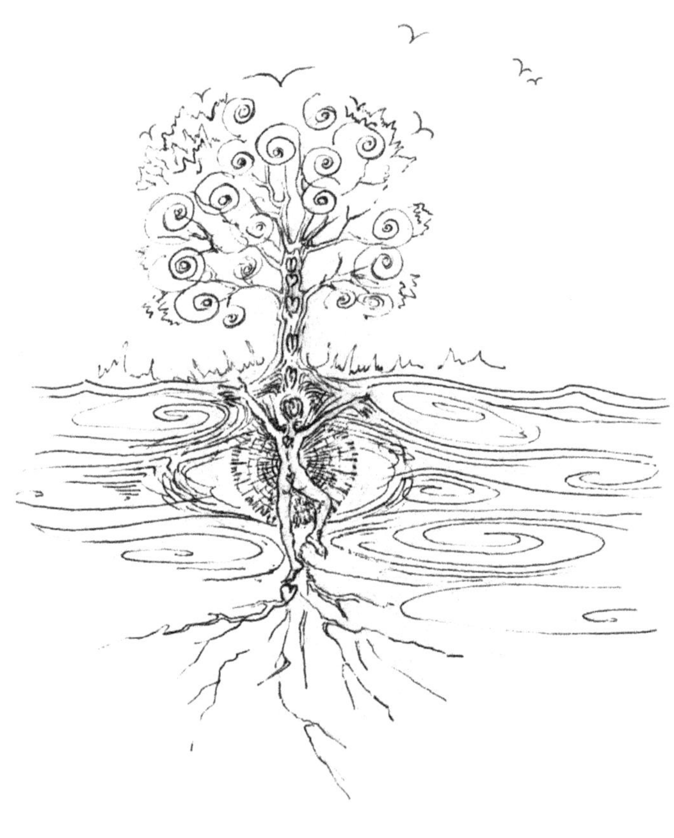

HOLY INCANTATION OF SOLACE

May love pour through our soul
weaving us together as One

May light flower in our heart
lending us the Grace to transform all fear

May warmth radiate our belly
bringing prosperity to all

May purity shimmer in our bones
filling us with the essence of the stars

May kindness resound in our voice
softening the path that lies ahead

May clarity shine through our mind
as we rest in the arms of the infinite

May solace abound in our life
touching all who we meet

May solace abound in the world
bringing all beings into perfect union.

PRAYER OF THANKS

Thank you, my Lord, my face
for pouring into me
for ladling your love into my heart.

Thank you for each happening in my life
for offering me the chance
to pocket your Grace.

Thank you for waiting for me
when I forget who I am
and even when I forget you.

Thank you, my Lord, my heart
for constantly cradling me
in your tender mother's arms
and for each day of my life
in this luminous world.

Thank you, Thank you, Thank you.

PRAYER OF RECONCILIATION

Our Lady,
who binds together
all things
and all beings
in all the worlds,

we pray for your help
to bring together
that which appears to be split.

We place our sweet wishes
within the tender womb of your heart.

May you wrap us in your eternal love,
May you clean this aching wound
with the waters of forgiveness,
May you heal this divide
with the holy balm from your hands.

And may the Songs of your heart
become the Songs of our Reunion,
May all beings be restored to original Purity,
May all beings rejoice in the field of your Praise
May all beings be unified in your infinite Peace.

PRAYER OF TRANSITION

Deep spirit of the eternal waters
Lord and Lady of Life and Death
we offer homage to you in this time of intense change
we bow to the great mystery of this unfolding
and breathe a deep sigh, yielding at last
to the sweet inevitability of Grace.
May we enter the gate with our hearts open
May we softly release the past
and open fully into the glory of your light.
May all who are caught up in this change
find the easy path to their highest good.
Great and ancient Grandmother of the Earth
we convey ourselves into your gentle arms.
Great, bright Lord of the blueing Sky
we release our soul to your boundless winds.
May all beings be blessed
May all beings be blessed
as together we journey
out of the darkness,
and like the leaping salmon
May each of us return
to the exquisite and inextinguishable
Flame of our Source.

SUPPLICATION OF DIVINE RAPTURE

Shatter my heart, O rapturous God,

crush me in the infinite softness of your embrace.

Lead me gently to the sacred shore

and drop me into your glittering depths.

Let the sword of my longing

pierce the rough hide of the Great Illusion

and may the blood of my life pour out

into the Sea of Eternal Creation.

By your Holy Grace,

May the Red Buddha sweep me clean -

leaving me stainless, pristine as diamond

Empty and Silent as the spotless sky.

O most Serene Lady of Limitless Bliss!

I court divine annihilation in your arms.

Pulverise my soul into luminescent dust

and scatter my dreams among the stars.

I bow to your thrust, to the Divine Rapture

that swells and wells in my breast

as you carve and shape my yearning soul

in the immortal fires of the Fervour of God.

INVOCATION OF THE ILLUMINATI
FOR SYNARCHY AND HARMONY

Beings of the higher worlds,

I salute you. I seek to align myself

with the highest harmony of the heavenly realms.

I make all seven layers of my being available

as a harp for your blessed fingers.

Please attune and bring into harmony

the multicoloured strings of my Self.

(Pause)

In deep harmony with the Ideal of Heaven on Earth,

I align myself with the Great White Brotherhood

I align myself with the Great Sapphire Sisterhood

I align myself with the Planetary and Celestial Synarchy

May my vehicle be used as a blueprint

for the incarnation of this great Ideal

May the beings from higher evolutions work through me,

bringing Grace and harmony to all that I do.

81

BLESSING OF THE ANGELS OF THE FIVE ELEMENTS

Angel of Earth, please purify my physical body *(3 breaths)*

Angel of Water, please purify my astral body *(3 breaths)*

Angel of Air, please purify my mental body *(3 breaths)*

Angel of Fire, please sanctify my spirit *(3 breaths)*

Angel of Ether, please gather the quintessence *(3 breaths)*

OPTIONAL MOVEMENTS

The arms lie open at your sides and gradually form a great arc as you reach up to the sky. Your palms come together above your head just as you summon the Angel of Fire and as you sanctify your spirit, your palms come down to rest in prayer position over your heart. Finally, as you summon the Angel of Ether, your hands come to rest face down on your belly.

THE LADY'S PRAYER

Our Lady, who lives at the heart of all form,
Hallowed be thy name.
May thy Queendom come,
May thy Will be done
that heaven may come to earth.

Please allow me this day
to drink from your sacred, silver spring
and forgive me my forgetting
as I learn through your Grace
to return all non-love with Love,

and take me by the hand
and lead me step by step
into the patient valley of your Heart

for yours is the earth,
my body and my life
for ever and ever
Amen.

BLESSING OF BIRTH

Great Beings of Infinite softness and truth
We salute you.
We entreat you to witness this birth.
May your manifold blessings shine forth
Upon the brow of this, our new beloved.

May the fruits and mellow seasons of the earth
Rain down upon this little life
Inspiring a lifelong journey of reverence and wonder.

Please protect and nourish this,
Your precious seed
As it falls and rises and learns and grows
In this, our dawning world.

May the great steadfast oak of your love
Offer peaceful, daily umbrage to this soul
As she weaves her dream
Into the waking hearts
Of the people of this world.
May the spirits of tree and plant and flower and star
Of wind and waves and distant mountain,
And all the creatures and elements of this earth
Inspire you little one…
May they be your constant companions
And may you serve them well,
As they shall serve you.

And as your life sprouts
And your soul's true purpose
Echoes round the valleys of your life,

May your roots plunge deep
May your path run smooth,
May your friends be many
May you find your sacred partner
May you face all storms
With the heart of the rose
And the valour of the lion.
And may the winds of wisdom
Loosen the leaves of your dreams
As you offer your gifts to the world.

And May the tender cradle of your family
fill you with vigour and the gentle faith
That all is well in this life.
May your every cell remember this truth
As you step forth from this day onwards.
May you carry the blessings of the Ancient Ones
May your life be blessed
By the sacred Mystery of the Three.

(anoint the head with 3 drops of pure water)

We offer these gifts as a sacred talisman
May they too be blessed.

(blessing the gifts)

We weave these circles around your head
And close our eyes to bow
In sacred Veneration.

(silence)

May your life be blessed.
May you help bring an end to all suffering.
May you realise in this very life
The Eternal Truth of your origin.

We give great thanks for your birth.
We give great thanks to our ancestors
And ask that they watch over you
As you shine your light in this world.

May your life be blessed
May your family be blessed
May all families be blessed
May all beings be blessed.

Amen.

For more information about Richard Rudd's
other books and the Gene Keys visit: